WINTER TENOR

WINTER

ALICE JAMES BOOKS | FARMINGTON, MAINE

TENOR

KEVIN GOODAN

10 9 8 7 6 5 4 3 2 1

Alice James Books are published by Alice James Poetry Cooperative, Inc.,
an affiliate of the University of Maine at Farmington.

ALICE JAMES BOOKS
238 MAIN STREET
FARMINGTON, ME 04938

www.alicejamesbooks.org

Library of Congress Cataloging-in-Publication Data

Goodan, Kevin, 1969–
 Winter tenor : poems / by Kevin Goodan.
  p. cm.
 ISBN-13: 978-1-882295-75-3
 ISBN-10: 1-882295-75-7
 I. Title.

PS3607.O563W56 2009
 811'.6—dc22

                    2009001740

Alice James Books gratefully acknowledges support from individual donors,
private foundations, the University of Maine at Farmington and the National
Endowment for the Arts. ❦

COVER ART: Carlo Ferrario (1833–1907)
"Winter Landscape"
LOCATION : Museo Francescano Missionario, Reggio Emilia, Italy
PHOTO CREDIT : Alinari/SEAT/Art Resource, NY

ACKNOWLEDGMENTS

The author would like to thank the editors and publishers of the journals and anthologies in which passages from this book first appeared, sometimes in different form: *Colorado Review, From The Fishouse, Lyric, The Massachusetts Review, Poems Across The Big Sky, Poetry Daily, and Poetry Quarterly.*

CONTENTS

Yet he was stalked by bush and beast

—Georg Trakl

WINTER TENOR

From here, the mare plodding forward
Is not important. Beyond the paddock
Trees unmitigated by laurel,
Birch yellow against the field-ice,
Blonde clouds at four P.M. that set crows
To elm and silence.
The mare is beside you and won't
Leave you alone. She knees
The steel gate of the barn, gnaws
The twine-fashioned latch. But geese
Over the far soil coax the air
For landing, and two steers
Nudge each other and bawl toward feed.
The mare won't leave you alone.
The derivative light of the fields
Is brightening, miasma
Sifts the trees, the ditch, the river
Aromatic from the fires.
The mare rubs her neck against your shoulder
And you smack her away—
The pneumatic sigh hoaring
The long, unshaved hairs of her snout,
Her great-roomed eyes—
You punch her nape but she does not shy.
It is then you hear blood puddling the snow.

The Lord is my shadow,
My shadow a land
That pleads every passage.
Mares graze, thunder-colored—
Weather's silent vanes.
The land sleeps, the rain and rivers merge—
How will I master the green language
Of the trees,
The fallowing, feraling,
Heralding of light,
These hands judged to labor?
Every post in the field has darkened.
A dove unfolds, folds back.

The mare in the front pasture is withering
And will not live to winter,
Which is a language I know,
The accuracy by which I am made,
Round pen full of weeds, burgeoning sentences
Of the fields, poplar that are verbs
For wind, a comma sizzling on bright tin
That is the body of a nestling dropped by a hawk—
The tolerances between which we almost prevail,
How any goat announces the arrival of something unseen.

To crave what the light does crave
To shelter, to flee
To gain desire of every splayed leaf
To calm cattle, to heat the mare
To coax dead flies back from slumber
To turn the gaze of each opened bud
To ripe the fruit and rot the fruit
And drive down under the earth
To lord a gentle dust
To lend a glancing grace to llamas
To gather dampness from fields
To divide birds
And divide the ewes from slaughter
And raise the corn and bend the wheat
And drive tractors to ruin
Burnish the fox, brother the hawk
Shed the snake, bloom the weed
And drive all wind diurnal
To blanch the fire and clot the cloud
To husk, to harvest,
Sheave and chaff
To choose the bird
And voice the bird
To sing us, veery, into darkness

White days, a passion for winter-birds
Cached in every elm, each goat
With its bell in the pasture
As wind tolls through the landscape,
A far gray band of willows,
The snow cross-harrowed, a barn
Where every breath has faltered
Where beasts lie down in stalls
Quiver and still, are hauled
To the fire, roil, and enter the earth
As wind skurls bright smoke
Against the purple that is darkness blooming

Strict land, stricter yet the wind shearing trees, patina that is November, dank clods stunned by ice. Where the light is no shadow goes and where wind, animals hunch and shimmer and are a storm's augury. Sing nones, sing vespers, send every message through fire like mares reined toward slaughter. I remember no birds, manes of cloud dissipating above an orchard where migrants flailed on ladders. Wind hawed their sing-ing, and come frost they too were gone. Fence wire snapped and barbs tore flesh of herds driven to the valley. My flesh was that flesh, as rivers divulged heat, turned solid. As I lease my body to crisp air, bright barns, the disheveled conspiracy of flocks now fleeing. Sing nones, sing vespers for what night does when fire fades. Ephphetha, be opened—

Pigeon blood drying on the shit-spreader.
Field rough-ploughed but not yet worked.
Arterial chill strafes each tree in my eyes,
The blanched hives in the rafters, bee-less,
Scent of weeds burnt before hard rain, soft rain,
The real rain abating. Birds come close, veer—
Are you not my hawk, my furrow?
Clouds mount the far hills, the ewe ketotic
On her side beneath a fir, the soiled humps
That are the heave and thrash of winter
Dying. All I know is that the Lord does not
Arrive straightforward, but as a thin halo of flies,
Grass greening against its will.
I gather dark buds from branches
And say I too could start with fire.
That the earth could torch every blossom
If it had to, and go on.

How will you know me
If you arrive in the dark
Thirty lanterns sway the field
Satellites shimmer in abeyance to stars
I am there you will find me
Give me thorns and I will praise
Thorns that is how I know
I'm yours divide me not
And I will bear the truncheon
Announcing our arrival

Miasma, the darkened river
Everything I know
In the mode of leaving
Steady pall of hayrick
Hoarse pleas of weaning lambs
Nudging at the gate
I put my hand in the ditch
Touched the shallow water
The land bright
But the fence not
My hand was cold, I could hear
The river, the trains—
It was then I came tacking
Through thistles, followed the fences
At the oak tree pushed a penny
In the mud, I heard other voices
But they were not my lambs,
I heard other voices,
There were thistles in my shoes
Briar cuts on my hands
When I stood in the river
There were lanterns further
I knew not, I waited,
I hit upon a song and skipped
A humming rock, the song
Went out of me, the trees

Toward night, frail flurries of snow. Fingernails of willows scratch frost from the kitchen window where I watch the field beyond the fence where once corn stood taller than a man but now I gaze into the kitchen of the next farmhouse and watch the man with a bad leg hobble from sink to table, feed his mother with a spoon. I keep the lights off and study snow to augur from the flakes what fortune I may. The furnace does its duty and cars pass, swirls of flurry captured in red prisms. If I stood on the road it would glow and crackle beneath my feet. The air would be muted, my own breath sounding as though it came from another body, a shadow leaning faintly toward me as though to whisper any comfort. Animals would unshelter themselves to stand waiting at the fence. Snow would settle everything. I cup my hands, realizing I have become what it was I wanted to be. The body beside me breathing on. The two of us.

Afterbirth hanging in the elm,
The vacant flag of my country—
As soil recalibrates simple desire,
Pollen becomes incident,
Light pealing against a few pale leaves
A mute flock turning and turning,
Begging danger. Bloodied pasterns
Of the heart, to what place do you will me
For what is the earth but a thing
To make time visible
And what is there, finally, to hold—
The ewe gone hoarse from bleating,
The lamb in me not singing to be saved.

And yet, to be lifted beyond any bounty
Is to no longer be
In utility with the Lord
As wind expedites the hours into dust—
A stubble-field into which
Black rain falls. It is known
That the wicked shall be known
As preachers of beauty,
Tenderness, as brightness hurries a bird
Toward singing,
For does not the sun bear down
Upon every shadow
With great purpose? The pollen
Is thick and the clouds
Dark at the far end of the sky.
The gust furrows,
And what heart does not reside in failure?

The first sturdy bee begins
To cross-pollinate the few flowers
Opened around the house.
It is March seventy degrees.
Last week saw snow on the ground.
A mosquito siphons my arm
And I do not smash it, stunned
As we are by being here.
Four lambs were born
And one is in the recycling bin
Dying. The ivy didn't
Survive the last hard cold spell.
Some things believed to be hardy
Are not so. And if there is danger,
If no world lasts
Who's to say we were even here at all.

Winter wheat is shorn
Between pours of rain
As the ram is held at bay
And income from the flocks is divided
Though nothing be a bumper-crop
And even wear-bars are threadbare.
I weld no skaggs for the harrow
Nor grant free-lease to rock doves
From barns wrapped in plastic.
This is evening now.
A foal grazes solitary in the front pasture
As weeds overtake the feedlot.
I hear the river, and your hand
Brushes against what is orphan in me.
The crecks of magpie do not behold me.
Dry sounds of starlings overhead,
Moon in halves beyond that.
As though I should have some answer.

The day spools up its turbines of light,
Systematic rupture of rock doves
From roofs, the fresh plowed
Weed-break at field's end, sweet stalks
Coming into corn where the truest augury
Is a kingbird in the mind.
Across the mitigation a birch-crushed wire
The heifers still obey
And a New Holland thresher keels its crop,
Splaying bright particulates to the air—
Weeds at full mast, crows fielding
For a lamb strapped to a post for bait—
A near hammer chipping slag from skaggs
Of a harrow, a duck's call echoes
In a valence we cannot hear like a river
Across bedrock, the ricket fence
That keeps this heart from the others.

Came blizzard came lambs stillborn
Came ravens cawing from pine
Snow hazarding every breath shadows
Lost their balance fled a lantern
Lighted but light is lost
In whiteness the stamping ewes
Coo around dark stains
Every direction overwhelmed bodies
Iced-up cawing

Some vireos working toward rapture in distant oaks, as I taste pollen when I breathe, as last night's rain works slowly through grass. A mist that gleams the skin of everything rises from black dirt of fields, and I, a slow traveler standing near a fire that smolders and chuffs and rekindles. Every small leaf has emerged, every flower. Oxen in the front pasture shoulder the fence, chewing the last sprigs of the last round-bale from winter. Soon they will labor with earth by day, by night. I count on my hands until darkness, hum each mile of travel. A blackness smolders in my throat though I am shining. I gather my knapsack of blades, my seed, sprig of ivy between my teeth. I walk to the trees where I've lodged my chariot, my flaming nag. A covey of pigeons pass over, a wind is mounting from the west where bright squares of rapefield curtsy and right, their bones filling with marrow. Sheep graze, blat for their kin that come rucking through bramble into this hour, this light, this ardor. This.

Snow-pits on discarded tin.
A dark herd wends and warps
In a far brightness that is the urge
And template, blurred by the passing
Of many wings. The gelding comes close,
Stales between its legs
As the chain tightens around the chest
Of a bloating heifer
And the tractor guns its smoke black
To lift and to ferry the body
To the bone-pit by the river
Where the flood will take it downstream
In a fortnight. I touch the breath
Of the gelding and think
Of the heifer's eyes unglazed
Swinging between heaven and
Heaven's heaven.

Even so, what hardships are bred
Into man are no different than the world—
Hair on the fence where fox
Wriggle through, sparrows
Nesting in the track of a sliding barn door
Hives dead in the eaves like sunflowers
Turned away from sun
Air rippling of so many wings,
You with your miscarriage, me
With my life, the crows that come,
As the ram butts a ewe around
To prime her for breeding,
As the barn door slides shut
Air stills again
I turn to the sun, to where you are—
Crushed birds, bright barns, glory

Ducks in a daze with mourning doves—
Sweetness of hay fresh mown, the clouds
Slowly stacking, the constant
Revectoring of flocks among weeds,
A dampness to northern aspects of field
Slanting toward the river, workmen
Silent, workwomen finding shade, what remains
Of harvest not mattering as one thing bears down
Upon the other—wind in ornamental trees,
The waxy mane of the whitest mare, whitest
From oncoming weather-light—
The foal not shying from the hand that gelded it.

Sheltered beasts shuffle back and forth in their bodies for warmth. The air crackles. No moon. Further out, steam rises from the opened belly of a lamb, ravens blood-lusting in the tree-hem, one ewe calls from safety, others wedge against their mother's ribs, turning and turning. The lamb's snout is bright with froth in the last shivers of departure as the air is needled with the reek of ruptured offal, the click of sharp teeth. Blood puddles at the base of a thistle, every platelet hungry for the earth, but the ice is deep and jealous, retaining the print of a coyote's foot like a seal upon a message from the king.

Clouds lenticular and birdless.
Pollen sheening the tepid air,
Dark shapes darting in the stagnant
Weedy water of a ditch, drying tufts
Of a rabbit chosen by a hawk,
As humidity seeps from contoured swaths
Across the belly of a hill.
Where rusted fence lay rent
Bulky lambs nudge each other
Into thistle and dead furrow and wheat.
To have watched the dandelion
Open its mane to sun, walked the river-shore
Its herons like witching sticks on dark water,
And sat as the groundchuck perused
Pigweed and cheetgrass in the pasture
Is to know death is a place
And each thing lives there. The deer
Among alder rakes flicking an ear
And not fleeing, ewes bleating
And not bleating for lambs beyond the proper gate.

You came winter behind you
All night wind shook the wood door
Don't be afraid you said I heard
Voices calling far off then nothing
Heard hands against the window
Saw fields with frost
Saw ewes bedded saw you
Light a candle place it in your mouth
No more I said no more
Room the color of skin from inside

A lamb nibs grass
Between the leg-bones
Of its predecessor,
Some cry from nonexistent
Clouds, some law
Of diminishing concordance,
The herd mentality
We are part of, God
Is part of, penned
In whatever darkness
We do not believe—
To harken, to wake
Resident, to dream
Which is the difference
Between one ewe
Rising in danger
And one ewe
Standing in hunger,
Or the freezer lambs
Calling to the unchosen—
From here you cannot follow

From the far ditch I believe in,
Crust of now cracking
In warrant of this broad hour
For which I plead, breathless
And unhawked from on high
And here on the floodplain
There is nothing that cannot
Seize me, cannot sunder—
My lord, my cyst, my lesion

Vesper sparrows flock and chant
Around the ewe kicked to death by mares.
The body not yet stiff, but bloated
And hostess to a thick peppering of flies—
Snout trampled, both eyes caked with dust.
I pick her up by the legs
And the mess of her body soaks through
The denim to my flesh. For a time
No sheep come into the shade,
Then one beds down in the blood.
I put the body in a wheelbarrow,
Leave a note on the barn for the coyotes
Or the owners, whichever come first.
At night my leg glows, an ember.

Whomsoever is in your house
Becomes your house.
And yet, how much can a body
Accommodate
For one must suffer torsion
To break into the light.
For now, it is summer.
From Lords Valley
To Dingmans Ferry I watch
Humidity ride open ground,
These stones, this field
Not lodged with what-has-been
But what-is-being—
The obese donkey nudging a fence
Waiting for news of any brother,
A rock wall entering a pond,
A burning log-deck,
Siamese cat in the mow-path
Crouching before the blades,
The overgrown road leads
To your house, wild dogs
Keep me to this path
And not another
For my god is not calmness
But a stand of birch
Catching flame

As I try to decide what is noun from verb
In the lark's fluted throatings—
Breaking the skin
Of each word I write.

And I remember the cry of peacocks and red paint fresh on the grain-barn, lethargic cones of grease on the zerks of the Farmall tractor idling in the mouth of the hayshed where the Desoto, Edsel, and the bird-limed Packard slowly grow back into the soil, the bull with cancer in its eye nudging the pickup for hay, dark strands of baling wire thrown in a bin by a bench that smelled of kerosene and wheat and antiquated boxes of parts for machinery no longer owned. In the burn-barrel wings and breasts of many birds were glazed and dotted with the crushed heads of kittens found mewling in the spaces between bales, crusted cans of Schlitz, hollow cardboard quarts of Quaker State Oil turned to fuzz by the frictive action of ice, fresh red spouts of Heet, all waiting to merge in that slow burning alchemical blaze as peahens in their piti-ful dun pecked the earth, starlings regrouped in the leafless bones of a poplar and a three-legged coyote sniffed the air at the far end of the field and found nothing to desire and hopped on

To watch the Northern Lights
Flare and recede,
Stench of cattle in the cooling air—
To consider the fields
Have nothing left to give—
Sparse birds of which I am one,
Briar that resides in me,
An ear toward harvest,
As I wait for you,
Who trod my flesh with light.

As I walk among lambs
With a bucket of knives,
As geese signify weather,
As a hawk strikes down,
As sparrows divide
And restitch morning,
The ewe prolapsed and panting
Beneath the trees,
The field that is now a lake,
The constant compression
Of wind through maple
As three mares unbed to graze
As mourning doves vie for the air,
As the far brush reddens,
As each being thrives, electric,
Blood pistons the ear

Today the light is beautiful. There is no other way to say this. I listen to Adam singing in the weeds. He stares at the sun, flicking his fingers before his pale eyes. When the military transport planes circle above his house, he claps and jabs out his arms as though assumed among their ranks. I yearn to be a sycamore standing in this kind of glaze, though bare and shorn of leaves. I could withstand the season for moments like this: to place every faith in the commerce of the windbreak, to shed vast sorrows at the arrival of a season. Adam is drooling and twisting sprigs of knapweed in his hair, and on the other side of the yard, a pit-bull is dozing. The boy has dirty roots clinging to the spaces between his teeth, as though he is going to blossom in the light.

I rise to sounds of labor: tractors in the fields, Jamaicans singing to harvest. Steam rises in tender strands from birch along the road, a foliate mess of dark birds flocking to the light. I walk the fence and watch. Moisture in my body rises through skin and sits there. Vapors clog my lungs. When I cough birds scatter, men look up from their toil and I wince. There are things I remember that brought me here, things I wanted to learn. The sun is hot and the sheep-fence electric in my hands. The men turn their backs and sing into the green rows. When I open my mouth, blackness becomes my eyes. There are freckles on the backs of my hands, on fingers between scars. I did not know I had been marked by light. Tractors go by on the road, empty then full, singing then silent as the last bin in the barn is hung. What is left is unfit for travel.

Beechnut burrs cast into fire,
Turkey wheat surging any field,
What will bushel, what will barrel,
The runnels bright where crops do flail—
And the tupelo has borne much fruit about her,
The wild state of common barberry,
Early in an early place—
That my intelligence belongs to field,
The wood-pewee telegraphing cloud-burst,
Blurry shift of aligned and unaligning stars—
What I want is to breed true the light,
The sweet gale fruit, beggar ticks
I carry with me, shrub-oak acorn cups
Empty but not fallen, some time frame
By which I shall not leave, the past
A rust mite among piles of leaves,
And as fire clears its throat
And claims a hunger, to take a thing
And make it whole again.

Sudden shock of field-surge after rain
Some lineage of wind that isn't broken
Some redbreast worming
As pollen engenders the air
Badger skull still clinging to flesh
Some weakness that remains in me
Cross-grained in a pasture not granted
Sheep-fence brittle with rust
Birds I see but cannot name
As I hold the Cheviot lamb
That will not feed against my thigh
Scratch its neck so it lifts its head
Saying random words in a soft voice
Until it closes its eyes and I pass
The blade across the neck quick
Systolic arcs surge from the kerf
Callnotes to the soil I'm not saying

The shrike that impales none
By some obscure faith,
A disorder not chaos
But a question of division
As dew, crestfallen
Shrinks from weeds and maples continue turning
Though it's only July—
There are roads not to take
Though the flood has passed
And heat comes on,
When to see any limited form
Is to not see—
Two notes that can always be heard—
Swallows above mud-slake,
No-see-ems in the heart,
Little knots of fire.

To be blessed with utility, like two mares
Deep in the chest, or a lamb thigh bone
Cracked for marrow, but what comes
Of this bounty if nothing is granted
Save the failing aleatorics of any flock
And the truth derived of damage—
That the laws at least of light prevail
Though it is only a vibration in air,
This pasture becoming my own, into which
I place nothing that is not already there—
Crows that come bismerian in burgeoning break,
Clod-sheen to the fields unharrowed,
Grass afire, banter of the mating finch
We who move forward as if we know—
The death I find standing
Where we are standing.

Crickets, thinly, last morning of summer. No frost yet, but soon. The dead aren't going anywhere, though the lathe in me keeps turning down the past. Water flows according to its nature and we are meant to yearn, to sigh, to loathe such easy beauty. Like the yellowjacket nests I prog, smash in the grass. The way they begin rebuilding the moment after.

For three weeks turkeys in the clearing
At dawn and dusk. First
Many chicks, and finally
The few. Large drops thwap dust
From the back of the donkey
As he enters the barn,
Dungheap burgeoning with weeds.
To step between the wires
And be the transference of the charge
Upon which every grace deceives me,
A strike among trees
In a place you do not live
In a body you do not have—

I'm back on the vision-deck
Feigning for the light.
Husk of August. What stands
In the distance glazed
With salt. Smell the body,
Taste the body. Cardinals
In the cheetgrass plead rain,
Each weed clump, every cracked leaf
Accounted for, freshed by the searing.
O verb of verbs, shape me, bless me,
O weal and woe draw the fire deeper
As veins of coal flame endless—
Green roots, speak. Burn me, gall me,
Drive me through.

Who will angel what remains?
Winter birds sing in every copse.
Canebrake, unknown star—
Old leaves burn
As if maple knew nothing more
Than rain. Such fleshly ardour
The dark urge we beatify—
A farmer turns his collar to the flame.
The sun idles down,
A storm makes dark in the east,
I whisper *brother,*
Come near my fire, we who saw
And sought, who bodied
And birded and lit
In the darkness. The corn
And windchill lend parity
To the clay. Llamas tarry the silage.
Will you go as gently to the knives?
The mares maintaining distance from the hedge-ditch.
And if I could sing. Every branch a branch of fire.

RECENT TITLES FROM ALICE JAMES BOOKS

Alice James Books has been publishing exclusively poetry since 1973. One of the few presses in the country that is run collectively, the cooperative selects manuscripts for publication through both regional and national annual competitions. New regional authors become active members of the cooperative, participating in the editorial decisions of the press. The press, which historically has placed an emphasis on publishing women poets, was named for Alice James, sister of William and Henry, whose fine journal and gift for writing went unrecognized within her lifetime.

Typeset and Designed by
DEDE CUMMINGS DESIGN
Brattleboro, Vermont

Printed by Thomson-Shore
on 30% postconsumer recycled paper
processed chlorine-free